Contents

Glossary.. 2

Christian worship through art....... 4

The story of Fra Angelico 6

Showing faith through colour 8

Meaning in stained glass............. 12

Symbols in Christian
   art and worship 14

Icons 18

Stations of the cross...................... 20

Representing people 22

Acting out faith.............................. 24

Using music in worship 28

Index.. 32

As you go through the book, look for words in **BOLD CAPITALS**. These words are defined in the glossary.

⚠ Understanding others

Remember that other people's beliefs are important to them. You must always be considerate and understanding when studying about faith.

Christian worship through art

Christians use many different types of art to show their faith.

People show their faith in many ways, for example, through prayer. But there are many other ways that people can express their faith.

◀ **Many statues show the resurrected Jesus as the 'Light of the World'.**

Art is anything that people create in order to express ideas, thought or feelings. Many people show their faith through arts such as painting, sculpture, drama or music. These arts can help us feel a certain way, such as happy or sad. They can also remind us of important things and teach us stories and ideas. Many religions also use colour and symbols to help teach important ideas.

For example, worshippers may sing songs which make them feel joyous and happy as part of worship.

Christians use many types of art to show their faith. Paintings, drawings, stained glass and statues of Jesus and of Christian saints help to make churches look beautiful and also tell stories of important Christians and events. Music and drama help bring religious feelings and stories to life. These arts also help worshippers to feel a certain way when we look, watch or listen to them. The colours, words and symbols used in these arts all help worshippers express their faith in different ways.

As you read through this book, you will have a chance to explore many of the different ways that Christians use the arts in the practice of their faith.

▼ An altar in a Catholic church with a painting of the Virgin Mary and baby Jesus, and Jesus crucified.

▲ A Fabergé Easter egg with a nativity scene – showing the birth of Jesus – inside.

The story of Fra Angelico

How one Christian artist felt about his art.

Angelico was born in the 15th century as Guido di Pietro, near Florence, Italy. He came from a well-to-do family and was trained as a portrait painter. However, he always longed to be a monk and he joined the Dominican order when he was in his early 20s.

Guido becomes Angelico

After he became a monk, he was called Fra Angelico. He continued to paint and draw, but instead of painting pictures of wealthy people, now all of his works of art had Christian subjects and were made to show the glory of God.

Every time he picked up a brush to paint, he would first offer a prayer to God, and every time he painted a scene of the crucifixion he cried.

Fra Angelico believed that painting was not just making beautiful pictures for decoration, but it should help others understand the glory and beauty of God.

A new way of painting

Fra Angelico's paintings were simple and realistic. He used colour, perspective, shading and landscape in order to make people feel a certain way. For example, in 1425, he painted a picture of Christ on the Cross. In this painting (shown opposite) he used very little colour, except for some red on the cross, on Christ's wounds and on thin lines of blood dripping from Christ's feet. The eyes of a person looking at this painting go to the red colour and the person is reminded of how Christ suffered on the cross.

Painting helps believers

Fra Angelico used colour, symbols and painting style in order to help people feel love towards God and Jesus. He was not the first artist to do this. Many other artists who have painted Christian subjects also do this. When you look at a painting or other Christian works of art, it is possible to see and feel what the artist wanted you to see and feel.

Fra Angelico died in 1455, and he was eventually made a saint in 1982.

◀ A 1425 painting by Fra Angelico of Christ on the cross. Showing Jesus' suffering helps worshippers to better understand God's message.

Showing faith through colour

Colours are used in Christian art to help worshippers understand Christian ideas.

Colour can help worshippers understand Christian ideas and even to know what is going on in a service

Colours of the seasons

Throughout the Christian year there are many different seasons and festivals, for example, Lent, Pentecost, Easter and Christmas. Each season and festival has its own colours. As the church seasons change throughout the year, the colours of the church decorations and of the minister's clothing also change. The different colours each have a special meaning and they help people to learn about that season or festival.

▲▼ Evergreen trees, such as pine and fir, are used in some cultures as a symbol of Christmas. The green reminds Christians of the promise of a new life with God. Red poinsettas are a reminder of the blood of Christ. The candle is a reminder of the light of God.

Church decorations

Churches are often decorated during the different seasons. These decorations may include clothes that are draped over the altar, banners that are displayed around the church, and other types of decoration.

The colours of the church decoration change with the church season. Each colour stands for something about that season. For example, black stands for death and mourning. It is used in many churches on Good Friday and Holy Saturday – the day when Jesus died and the next day. So, seeing black colours in church on these days, helps worshippers to feel sad for Jesus' death.

Fifty days after Jesus died on the cross, the apostles gathered for the festival of Pentecost. During the festival, the Holy Spirit came to the apostles in the form of fire, or flames, and helped them to perform miracles. So, during Pentecost many churches are decorated in red colours, or hang cloth

◀ A hanging with a red flame for Pentecost.

banners with flames on them, as a reminder of the first Pentecost and a symbol of the presence of God.

Some churches may be decorated in green branches during Advent and Christmas. Green is a reminder of the promise of new life. So the branches remind worshippers of how Jesus was born on Christmas.

The Advent wreath

The lighting of an Advent wreath is a familiar custom during this season in churches and in homes. A wreath is formed, usually of evergreen branches, and adorned with four purple or pink candles. A single white candle sits in the middle of the wreath. On each Sunday in Advent a new purple or pink candle is lit until, at last, all four candles are burning. The green of the evergreen branches stands for eternal life. The royal blue or purple candles stand for Jesus as King. Some churches attach other meanings to the four candles, such as hope, peace, love and joy. The increasing light shed by the candles represents worshippers' increasing joy as the day of Jesus' coming approaches. On Christmas Day the white candle is lit to proclaim that the Light of the World has come.

Colours in clothing

In many churches, ministers wear special clothing, called vestments. The colours of this clothing changes throughout the year. Changing the colours of their clothing is one way that some ministers help worshippers to understand the different seasons of the Christian year.

Royal blue and purple are colours that stand for royalty. In some churches, the minister wears these colours during Advent and Christmas, to welcome the coming of Jesus as King.

▼ Gold is worn for Christmas Eve mass as a reminder that Jesus is king.

White	White is for purity, holiness, virtue and respect. It is used at Christmas, Epiphany and Easter time, and also for baptisms, marriages and saints' days.
Gold	Gold is for majesty, joy and celebration. It also stands for the presence of God. At Christmas and Easter gold is sometimes worn.
Green	Green is for living things and the promise of new life. It is used between Epiphany and Lent, and between Pentecost and Advent.
Purple	Purple is for pain, suffering and mourning. It is the colour of Lent and funerals. As the colour of royalty it has also been used at Advent.
Red	Red is for fire and stands for the presence of God. It is the colour of Pentecost. Red is also the colour of the church, as it stands for the colour of the blood of Jesus Christ.
Black	Black is for death and mourning. It is used only on Good Friday and Holy Saturday before the Easter Vigil.

Royal blue is also a reminder of the night sky, where the star appeared to announce the birth of Jesus.

Ministers often wear white or gold at Christmas. White stands for purity, celebration and holiness while gold stands for something that is valuable and precious. These colours are worn at Christmas as a reminder that Jesus is King. Because gold is a bright and beautiful colour, it can also stand for feelings of joy and happiness.

11

Meaning in stained glass

Colours can help give special meaning to Christian works of art.

Stained glass has been used to teach people about the life of Jesus and about the Christian faith for many centuries.

One reason for having stained glass decoration is the belief that the beauty of the glass would bring worshippers closer to God.

As the light shines through the glass, the colours light up and remind worshippers of the light of God.

The colourful light is also a reminder of how, according to the Bible, God began to create the world with the words, "Let there be light". It is also a reminder of how Jesus described himself as "the light of the world".

▶ Mary in white, for purity, and her son, Jesus, in violet, who takes on the sins of the world.

Telling stories with colour

The colours used in stained glass windows can help to tell the story that is shown. For example, clear glass or yellow glass might be used in the background of stained glass showing apostles or saints, as a way to show that the light of God is shining on that person. Yellow is also used for halos as a way to show Heaven.

Colours can also stand for ideas, for example, white glass may stand for purity. Mary is often shown wearing white robes. Colour can also stand for feelings, for example red may stand for anger and violet may stand for love, or suffering.

In stained glass, rainbows stand for the way that God forgives our sins. For example, God sent a rainbow to Noah after the flood to show that the Earth was now cleansed of sin.

◄ A nativity scene showing Mary (in violet) and Joseph (both with yellow halos), and the baby Jesus in the manger. The scene is surrounded by a rainbow. This reminds worshippers that Jesus can forgive our sins.

Symbols in Christian art and worship

Like colour, special symbols can also add meaning to Christian works of art.

▼ This Baptism candle shows the chi-rho.

A symbol is a design, drawing or object that can have many different meanings.

The cross

The most important symbol of Christianity is the cross. The cross is a reminder of the death of Jesus. When Christians see a cross, or a picture of a cross in a work of art, they are reminded of how Jesus died and was taken to Heaven.

▶ Crosses on churches can be found in several different shapes, but they all have the same meaning.

The chi-rho ☧

A symbol you may find on the altar is made of two intertwined Greek letters. This is the chi-rho symbol. It is made up of the Greek letters chi (χ) and rho (ρ). These are the first letters of the Greek word 'XPICTOC' (pronounced Christos), which means 'Christ'. You can often see the chi-rho on banners, vestments, and candles as well. It is a reminder of Jesus Christ.

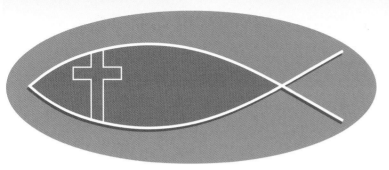

The fish symbol

A simple fish symbol, drawn with two lines, is a reminder of the Greek phrase "Jesus Christ, Son of God, Saviour". In Greek, the first letter of each word in the phrase makes up the Greek word ICHTHUS, which means 'fish'.

This symbol was used during the early years of Christianity, when Christian worship was illegal and Christians were often arrested, jailed and even killed.

Christians in those days used the fish symbol as a secret sign of their shared faith. One person would draw an arc in the sand, and the other would complete the sign to show his brotherhood in Christ.

Eagle

The eagle has many meanings. Because the eagle soars upwards, it stands for Jesus' rising up to Heaven after his death on the cross.

Eagles also stand for people who have been baptised. In ancient times, people believed that eagles grew new feathers by flying near the Sun and then plunging into a lake or fountain. So the eagle was also a symbol for the Resurrection, the rebirth of Jesus after his death.

The eagle also stands for the word of God. Carved statues of eagles are often found on pulpits, where they were originally used to hold open the Bible as the priest or minister read from it during the sermon.

▶ An eagle at the top of the cupola on the palace church at Petrodvorets, Russia.

Symbols, saints and apostles

In paintings Saint John the apostle is often shown holding a book. This is a reminder that he wrote the Gospel of John and the Book of Revelation in the Bible.

St Francis of Assisi is always shown wearing a very simple robe, tied with a plain cord with three knots. The three knots are a reminder that St Francis made three promises to God – poverty, chastity and obedience.

Apostles and saints are also usually shown with a halo above their heads. This is a sign that they have gone to Heaven. The circle of the halo stands for eternal life. Jesus is usually shown with a halo that has three parts. These stand for the three parts of God – the Father, the Son and the Holy Spirit.

A lamb may be used to stand for Jesus. This is because John the Baptist called Jesus the "lamb of God who takes away the sin of the world". In other works of art, Jesus is shown as a shepherd. This is a reminder of the way Jesus looks after all people, like a shepherd looks after his flock.

Even simple, everyday objects can have special meaning. For example, a gate, when shown open, may stand for the entrance to Paradise.

◀ St Francis of Assisi statue showing his simple robe with three knots, and the tamed wolf (see page 22).

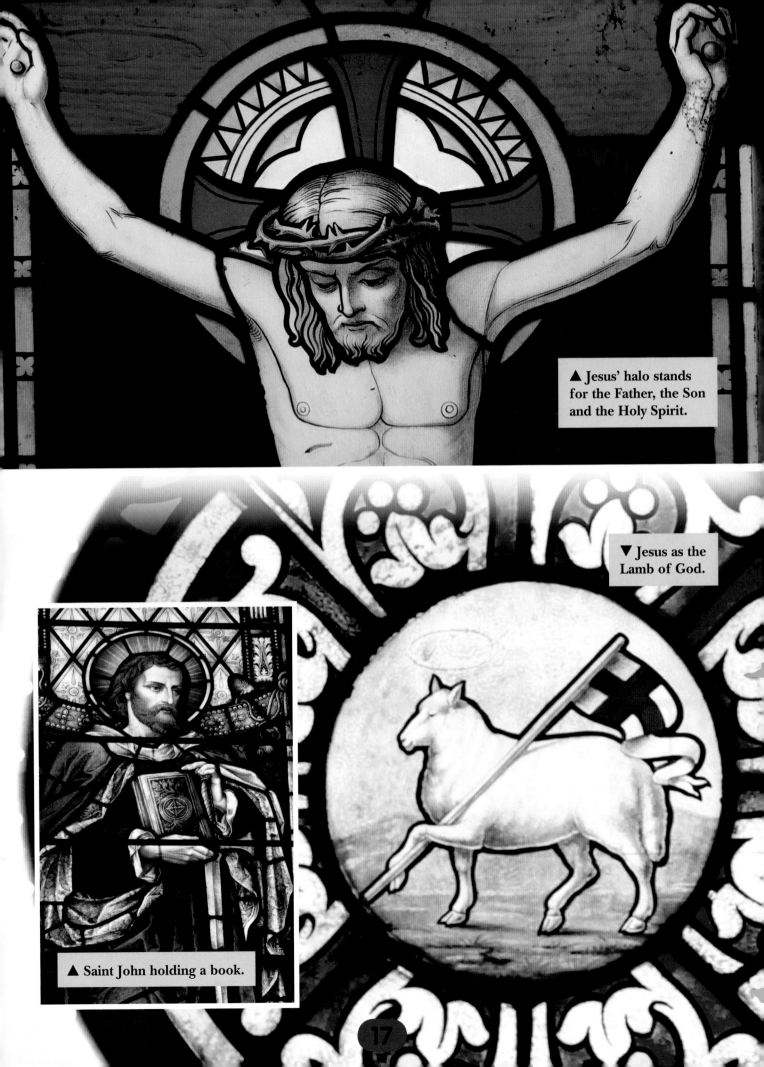

▲ Jesus' halo stands for the Father, the Son and the Holy Spirit.

▼ Jesus as the Lamb of God.

▲ Saint John holding a book.

Icons

Icons are paintings that are used to teach about important Christians.

In some types of Christian painting, artists use symbols and colours to give the painting extra meaning. This type of painting is called an icon. Icons usually show Jesus, the apostles or saints in very simple surroundings. They usually do not have plants or buildings or other people in them. Instead, icons use symbols and colour to tell us something about the person in the painting.

◄ This icon shows St George slaying the dragon. St George was a Turkish saint called Girgis. When the crusaders fought near Turkey in the Middle Ages, they began praying to him as their patron saint.

▼ The background picture shows a ceiling in a Greek Orthodox church with scenes from Jesus' life.

This is another common style of icon. It shows Jesus as a teacher, holding a book. Jesus has two fingers raised in a blessing. The two fingers also stand for Jesus' two roles, as teacher and spiritual leader. The letters 'ICXC' are short for 'Jesus Christ'. The halo over Jesus' head is divided into three parts, that stand for the three parts of God – the father (God), the Son (Jesus) and the Holy Spirit.

Below is a similar image of a saint, but in a different artistic style.

The icon painting on the left is of Mary and the infant Jesus. In the painting, Mary is looking down at Jesus. Both Mary and the infant Jesus look sad. This is to remind viewers that the infant will be crucified when he is an adult. The infant also looks like an adult – this is another reminder of what happens to Jesus as a man.

Both Mary and the infant Jesus have halos around their heads. The gold of the halos stands for the light of God. The Baby Jesus has two fingers raised in a blessing.

Jesus is condemned to death

▲ Station 1

Stations of the cross

The stations of the cross tell the story of Jesus' last days on Earth.

On the walls of many churches you will find 14 small plaques, statues or paintings called the Stations of the Cross. These are 14 things that happened to Jesus on his way to be crucified. Worshippers walk from one station to another. At each station, worshippers say the words, "We adore you, O Christ and we bless you, because by your holy cross you have redeemed the world."

Jesus receives his Cross

▲ Station 2

Jesus falls the first time

▲ Station 3

Jesus meets his afflicted Mother

▲ Station 4

Jesus speaks to the daughters of Jerusalem

▲ Station 8

Jesus falls the third time

▲ Station 9

Jesus is stripped of his garment

▲ Station 10

While they walk, worshippers may say additional prayers or think about Jesus and how he died. The plaques or paintings help worshippers to remember Jesus' suffering.

The pictures are a virtual way for worshippers to visit each of the sites of these events, which is what the early Christians were able to do.

The style of the pictures can also help worshippers to think about Jesus' death. For example, these are reliefs and they help to bring the pictures to life for the viewer, and make worshippers feel they are part of the story.

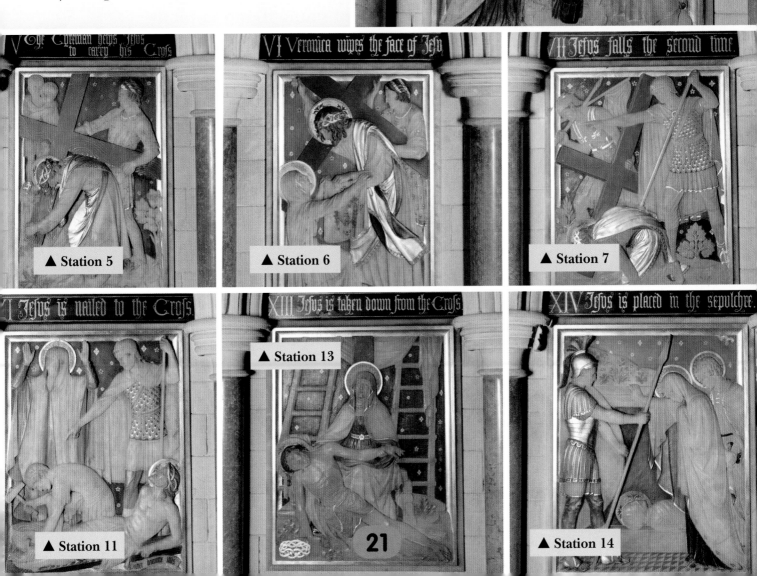

▲ Station 12

▲ Station 5

▲ Station 6

▲ Station 7

▲ Station 11

▲ Station 13

▲ Station 14

Representing people

Statues are used to teach about the lives of important Christians.

Statues of Jesus and the saints are most common in Roman Catholic and Orthodox churches and are used to help people to focus their thoughts on God.

For example, a statue of St Francis and a wolf may remind people of the story of how one day the people of the small town of Gubbio, in Italy, asked Francis to save them from a ferocious wolf (see page 16). All efforts to trap the wolf or drive him away had failed. When Francis found the wolf, he was not afraid. Instead, he began to pray and soon the wolf was tamed and followed Francis everywhere. This story shows that faith in God can help people to overcome danger.

Statues of the Virgin Mary holding the baby Jesus are also very common in some churches. As with the Stations of the Cross, worshippers may stand in front of the statue while saying prayers and thinking about the life of Mary.

Statues of events in the life of Jesus are also often found in churches. For example, statues showing the Last Supper or the baptism of Jesus serve the same purpose as other statues – they tell a story and are reminders of important events.

Effigies

Effigies are another type of statue found in many churches. The word effigy means 'likeness'. In early medieval times, important people would have stone likenesses of themselves carved to go on top of their tombs so they could be remembered. These tombs were then placed in the church so that they would be as close as possible to God.

◀ An effigy of an important person.

▲ This statue shows Christ's baptism by John the Baptist.

◀ This statue shows the Virgin Mary, Jesus' mother, and the baby Jesus in her arms.

▼ Many young children play the part of angels or shepherds in the school nativity.

Acting out faith

Putting on a play can teach people about Christian ideas.

From the earliest days of Christianity, drama has been used to teach worshippers about Jesus and the Christian faith. When a story is acted out, it can seem more real than when it is read from a book. So acting is a way of making the Bible stories come to life for worshippers.

Plays and dramatic readings have been used in this way since the first centuries of Christianity, when they were a common way to teach about Christianity. Today, plays are a fun way to involve worshippers in learning the stories of the Bible.

▶ In this church nativity, this man is playing the wise man bringing frankincense to the baby Jesus.

Nativity play

The word nativity means 'birth' and nativity plays tell the story of Jesus' birth. These plays are usually put on during Christmas, the holiday that celebrates Jesus' birth.

Many churches, and some schools, put on nativity plays, often starring children. Some of the scenes in a nativity play include: the angel Gabriel appearing to Mary; the trip to Bethlehem; the birth in the stable; the visit by the shepherds; and the visit by the three wise men.

▶ These children are playing the parts of Mary and Joseph in a school nativity. The doll is taking the part of the baby Jesus.

Passion plays

One meaning of the word passion is suffering, so a passion play tells about the suffering of Jesus. Passion plays tell the story of Jesus' last days and his death on the cross.

Easter is the Christian holiday that remembers Jesus' suffering and death, and so passion plays are put on during the period just before Easter. During a passion play, actors act out the story of Jesus' last days.

▼ Scenes from a modern dress passion play.

The arrest of Jesus.

Passion plays may be written and put on by churches, schools, drama clubs and Christian organisations. They are often performed outdoors.

Some of the scenes shown in a passion play are: Jesus riding into Jerusalem, the Last Supper, Jesus' arrest in the Garden of Gethsemene, Jesus' trial, the 40 lashes, Jesus carrying the cross to Calvary, Jesus being nailed to the cross, Jesus' death and Jesus' resurrection.

Mystery plays and miracle plays

Mystery plays act out stories from the Old and New Testaments of the Bible, such as the story of Adam and Eve, the story of Noah's Ark or the story of the raising of Lazarus from the dead.

In the Middle Ages, mystery plays were sometimes performed on special horse-drawn carts that would travel from town to town. The carts were called pageants and today this type of play is also sometimes called a pageant.

Jesus carrying the cross on his way to his crucifixion

The crucifixion of Jesus.

Today, some churches and Christian groups still put on modern versions of mystery plays to help worshippers understand the Bible stories.

Another type of play is called the miracle play. These tell the story of particular saints and the miracles they performed.

Mystery plays and miracle plays are most common in the Roman Catholic church.

▲ Jesus contemplates his own death in the garden of Gethsemene.

Jesus falling with the cross.

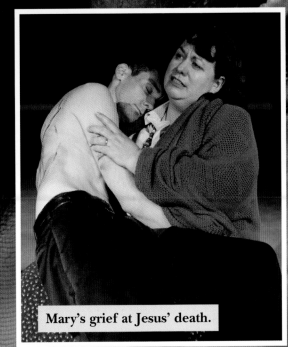

Mary's grief at Jesus' death.

Using music in worship

Music is used in worship in order to remind people of important ideals of Christianity.

Music is an important part of Christian worship. Different types of music may help worshippers to feel things such as joy, tranquillity, thanksgiving, awe, wonder or even sadness.

You can see this in the following story, which tells why one popular Christmas song, 'Silent Night, Holy Night' was written.

The story of 'Silent Night'

It is a few nights before Christmas Eve 1818 in Oberndorf, Austria. Father Joseph Mohr, the pastor at St Nicholas Church in Oberndorf, knows what he wants to say during his Christmas sermon, but he needs a special song to use during the service. While he is trying to think of a song, Father Mohr decides to take a walk.

As he walked the snow-covered streets of his village, Father Mohr felt that the peaceful town, covered by a white blanket of snow, seemed to be waiting quietly for the miracle of Christmas to arrive. He was reminded of a similar night long ago, when shepherds watched their flocks on the hillside above Bethlehem and the baby Jesus was born in a manger.

Standing in the snow the young pastor imagined the moments of that special night long ago. He thought of the poem he had written two years earlier and decided that it would make the perfect song for Christmas.

The next morning is Christmas Eve. Father Mohr took his poem to the church organist, Franz Gruber, and together they worked out a tune.

That night, Father Mohr played the tune on a guitar while the St Nicholas church choir sang 'Silent Night, Holy Night' for the first time. By the time the last notes died away, the worshippers were filled with joy and wonder at the song. The next day the song was being hummed and sung in all the homes around Oberndorf.

Silent night, holy night!
All is calm, all is bright
Round yon Virgin, Mother and Child.
Holy infant so tender and mild,
Sleep in heavenly peace,
Sleep in heavenly peace.

Silent night, holy night!
Shepherds quake at the sight.
Glories stream from heaven afar
Heavenly hosts sing Alleluia,
Christ the saviour is born!
Christ the saviour is born.

Silent night, holy night!
Son of God, love's pure light.
Radiant beams from Thy holy face
With the dawn of redeeming grace,
Jesus Lord, at thy birth,
Jesus Lord, at thy birth.

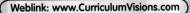

Songs with special meanings

You can see from the story of 'Silent Night' that the songs used in Christian worship can be used to celebrate and remember certain events. For example, 'Silent Night' helps worshippers to feel the awe and wonder of Jesus' birth.

Other songs may remind worshippers of important Christian ideals. For example, the song 'Swing Low, Sweet Chariot' was written in America in the 1800s. It reminds worshippers that God is always with them, even in bad times. In the past it was sung by slaves, and helped them to imagine that some day God would help them to be free. Here are some of the words:

Chorus: Swing low, sweet chariot
Comin' for to carry me home
Swing low, sweet chariot
Comin' for to carry me home

I looked over Jordan and what did I see
Comin' for to carry me home
A band of angels comin' after me
Comin' for to carry me home
(Chorus)

If you get to heaven before I do
Comin' for to carry me home
Tell all my friends I'm comin' there too
Comin' for to carry me home
(Chorus)

I'm sometimes up and sometimes down
Comin' for to carry me home
But still I know I'm heaven bound
Comin' for to carry me home
(Chorus)

Hymns

Some of the earliest types of Christian music were chants. Christian congregations would chant the psalms together during worship, using simple tunes. These were usually performed without any musical instruments.

Beginning in the 16th century, many new songs praising God – called hymns – began to be written. These were meant to be sung either by a choir or by the worshippers.

Some hymn writers used Psalms and also other parts of Bible scripture for the words. But many hymn writers used the meaning of the Bible rather than its exact words.

Tunes and instruments

The tunes and instruments used in Christian music all help worshippers to understand Christian ideals and feel closer to God. For example, one of the most famous types of instrument used in Christian music is the organ. The deep sounds of the organ inspire feelings of awe and wonder. Today, almost any type of instrument or tune may be used in church music.

Sometimes, a tune may be solemn and help people feel the awe, mystery and wonder of God. Other times, a tune may be faster, to help people feel happier.

▼ An organ in a church. The sound of the organ is deep and helps worshippers to feel a sense of awe and wonder.

Index

Advent 2, 9, 10
altar 9
apostles 2, 9, 13, 16, 18

baptism 10, 14, 15, 22
Bible 12, 15, 16, 27
black 9, 10, 11, 21
blue 9, 10, 11, 19

candle 9, 14
chi-rho 14
Christmas 8, 9, 10, 11, 28, 29
church 4, 5, 8, 9, 10, 11, 20, 26, 27, 29, 30
cross 7, 9, 14, 15, 20, 21, 26, 27
crucifixion 2, 5, 6

Dominican 6

eagle 15
Easter 2, 8, 10, 11, 26
Epiphany 2, 2, 10

festival 8, 9
fish 15
flames 9
Fra Angelico 6–7
frankincense 24

gold 10, 11, 19
Good Friday 2, 10
green 8, 9, 10, 19

halo 16, 17, 19
Heaven 13, 14, 15
Holy Saturday 10
Holy Spirit 2, 9, 17, 19
hymn 30

icon 18–19

Joseph 13

king 9, 11

Lamb of God 16, 17
Last Supper 22, 26
Lazarus 26
Lent 2, 8, 10, 11

manger 13, 25
Mary 5, 12, 13, 19, 22, 23, 25, 27
minister 8, 10, 15
miracle play 27
monk 6
mystery play 26, 27

nativity 2, 13, 24, 25
Noah 13, 26

Orthodox 2, 18, 22

pageant 26
passion play 26
Pentecost 2, 8, 9, 10
poinsetta 8
pulpit 15
purple 9, 10, 11

rainbow 13
red 9, 10, 11, 19
Resurrection 2, 15, 26
(Roman) Catholic 2, 5, 22, 17

St Francis 16, 22
St George 18
St John 16, 17, 23
season (in Christianity) 2, 8, 9, 10
stained glass 12–13
stations of the cross 2, 20–21, 22
symbol 2 *and throughout*

vestments 10, 14
violet 12

white 9, 10, 11, 12, 21
wreath 9

yellow 13

Curriculum Visions

There's much more on-line including videos

You will find multimedia resources covering six different religions, as well as history, geography, science and spelling subjects in the subscription Professional Zone at:

www.CurriculumVisions.com

A CVP Book
Copyright Earthscape © 2008

Author
Lisa Magloff, MA

Religious Adviser
Reverend Colin Bass, BSc, MA

Senior Designer
Adele Humphries, BA

Editor
Gillian Gatehouse

Acknowledgements
The publishers would like to thank the following for their help and advice:
St James Church, Muswell Hill, London;
St John the Baptist Church, Wightman Road, London; Father George Christidis of St Nictarios, Battersea, London; Rector Father Terence Phipps of St James Church, Spanish Place, London.

Photographs
The Earthscape Picture Library, except: (c=centre, t=top, b=bottom, l=left, r=right) *DreamTime* page 16; *ShutterStock* pages 1, 4–5, 8, 10, 11c, 12–13, 14–15, 17, 18–19, 23l, 24–25, 27 (main), 28–29; *TopFoto* pages 6–7.

Designed and produced by
Earthscape

Printed in China by
WKT Company Ltd

Christian art and writing
– Curriculum Visions
A CIP record for this book is available from the British Library
ISBN: 978 1 86214 247 3

This product is manufactured from sustainable managed forests. For every tree cut down at least one more is planted.

WORLD WAR II
Lost Words

COLIN HYNSON

KEY TO IMPORTANT ARTICLES

Look out for the following symbols through this book, highlighting key articles from the past.

FILM EXCERPT
Primary source material taken from a film about the subject matter.

SONG EXCERPT
Lyrics extracted from songs about the subject matter.

OFFICIAL SPEECH
Transcribed words from official government speeches.

GOVERNMENT DOCUMENT
Text extracted from an official government document.

LETTER
Text taken from a letter written by a participant in the events.

PLAQUE/INSCRIPTION
Text taken from plaques/monuments erected to remember momentous events described in this book.

INTERVIEW/BOOK EXTRACT
Text from an interview/book by somebody there at the time.

NEWSPAPER ARTICLE
Extracts taken from newspapers of the period.

TELEGRAM
Text taken from a telegram sent to or by a participant in the events.

Copyright © ticktock Entertainment Ltd 2005
First published in Great Britain in 2005 by ticktock Media Ltd.,
Unit 2, Orchard Business Centre, North Farm Road, Tunbridge Wells, Kent, TN2 3XF
ISBN 1 86007 836 2 pbk
Printed in China
A CIP catalogue record for this book is available from the British Library.